"Little did I know my suggestion to rewrite the Bible would light the fires that are burning with such intensity. The fires have reached such a high intensity that they are almost unquenchable. Nor should they be quenched" ~ Professor Canaan Banana

The Case For A New Bible

HOLY BIBLE

PROFESSOR CANAAN S BANANA

June 14, 1991

Author Biography

'Brief Background History of Canaan Sodindo Banana'

PRESIDENT CANAAN SODINDO BANANA

Canaan Sodindo Banana was born on March 5 1936 at Esiphezini, in Essexvale District, near Bulawayo, Southern Rhodesia. He was educated at a mission school, followed by Tegwani Teacher Training Institute and Epworth Theological College, where he was ordained as a Methodist minister in 1962.

He worked at various missions and was chairman of the Bulawayo Council of Churches in 1969-70 and of the Southern African Urban Industrial Mission from 1970 to 1973. He alarmed the authorities by publishing his own version of the Lord's Prayer, encouraging Africans to resist white supremacy.

Banana spent a year travelling in South-East Asia and Japan (where he took a diploma at Kansai Industrial Centre). On his return he became an active nationalist, joining the newly-formed African National Council (ANC), of which Bishop Abel Muzorewa was president. He became its vice-president and campaigned for the rejection of the agreement between Rhodesia's prime minister Ian Smith and Sir Alec Douglas-Home during the Pearce Commission inquiry.

In 1972, Banana accompanied Muzorewa on a visit to London to press for another constitutional conference. In consequence, Banana's passport was confiscated on his return, and he fled on foot to Botswana in 1973. He ended up in America on a three-year scholarship and studied for a master's degree in Theology at Wesley Theological Seminary, Washington DC.

On his return to Rhodesia in 1975, Banana was arrested at the airport and jailed for leaving the country without a passport. On his release in January 1976, he flew to Bulawayo but was kept under house arrest. Later in the year he was allowed to join Muzorewa's team at settlement talks in Geneva, during which he defected to Robert Mugabe's Zanu (the Zimbabwe African National Union).

On his return to Rhodesia in December 1976, he dismissed Muzorewa as "irrelevant and gullible" and the following year established the People's Movement to represent the internal wing of Mugabe's party. He was again detained, but was released shortly before Lord Soames arrived as Governor in 1979.

Banana became first president of an independent Zimbabwe on April 18 1980, when he received the constitutional instruments from the Prince of Wales. As a former political detainee and a member of the minority Ndebele people, he had impeccable political credentials, and was the only person nominated by Zanu.

Banana used the presidential platform to attack the churches for their mealy-mouthed approach to the liberation struggle, and in 1980 called for a "radical transformation" of the content of the Christian message: "When I see a guerrilla, I see Jesus Christ," he declared. Later, he suggested that the Bible should be rewritten to make it relevant to people in post-colonial societies.

In September 1980 Banana was an intermediary in talks about merging Zanu-PF and Joshua Nkomo's Zapu and was credited with brokering the 1987 Unity Accord which brought to an end the Matabeleland massacres in which Mugabe's army is thought to have killed an estimated 20,000 civilians.

Banana took a great interest in raising chickens at Mrs Banana's farming co-operative in the grounds of State House and acquired his own farm just outside Harare. Due to the Zanu PF Leadership Code all government officials were asked to stop using their positions to amass wealth and asked to dispose of any property they had purchased whilst in office, Banana converted his farm in Marondera to an Agricultural College and named it Kushinga Phikelela, now called Kushinga Phikelela Polytechnic. He sent Prince Charles a poem for his wedding, and wrote five books on theology and politics. His other interests included refereeing football matches, conducting a choir, and playing tennis and Ping-Pong.

The loss of office in 1987 was not without its compensations. Banana retired that year on very favourable terms, with a tax-free pension for life of £25,443, lifetime immunity from import duties, and with a secretary, two security guards and a vehicle allowance.

Thereafter he served, in January 1989, on the United Nations commission of eminent churchmen investigating business in South Africa. At the end of 1991 he led the World Council of Churches (WCC) "Eminent Church Persons" on sanctions against South Africa which observed Codesa (Convention for a Democratic South Africa) and was co-chairman of the UN panel conducting public hearings on the operations of transitional corporations in South Africa. He also played an active part, on behalf of the Organisation of African Unity, in seeking to broker peace in Liberia.

He married, in 1961, Janet Mbuyazwe and had three sons and a daughter (Michael Thabo Bekezela, Nathan Sipho, Martin Mhambi Salaam and Nobuhle). After standing by her husband during his trial, Mrs Banana left Zimbabwe for Britain, where she claimed political asylum after the continued humiliation and harassment that was created by the controversial case against her husband in a country they made sacrifices to liberate. She only returned to Zimbabwe after Mugabe was toppled by a bloodless coup in November 2017 in early January 2019.

THE

CASE FOR A NEW BIBLE

Professor Canaan S Banana

SEMINAR: RELIGIOUS STUDIES, CLASSIC AND PHILOSOPHY

LR 128

June 14, 1991   2:15 PM

THE CASE FOR A NEW BIBLE

by

Professor Canaan Sodindo Banana

"Let us admit the case of the conservatives: if we once start thinking no one can guarantee where we shall come out,except that many objects, ends and institutions are doomed.Every thinker puts some portion of an apparently stable world in peril and noone can wholly predict what will emerge in it's place".

Quoted by Ratner in his book " Intelligence in the mordern world" .p.v

On the 6th of April 1991, I had the priviledge to discuss the task of African (third world) theologians on the Middle east Question in Hatfield. As is well known, the Zionist administration eptimizes a trauma for Palestinian Arabs. The Arabs have known nothing but haunting experiences, harrowing nightmares and contemptuous disregard of human dignity from their history of alien administration.

If one looks at the Middle East situation he/she finds that something is seriously wrong and that something must be done to remedy the situation. Zionism is dangerously misguided by religious fundamentalism. Zionist regard themselves as a covenated people - the so-called "chosen people" - and thus divinely justified to take any action however horrendous in the name of religion. it is during this discussion that the idea of rewritting the Bible crossed my mind.

I challenged Christian scholars to seriously consider rewriting the Bible so that God can be liberated from dogmas that make him the property of ethnic syndicates. Zionism domesticates God and claims the mandate to perpertrate hooliganism in the name of the Bible. several questions clamour for attention. Does our infallable God legitimize the inhuman and brutal treatment of Palestinians? Is this God a national God? Is he not a universal God? Is he not God of justice and mercy?

Little did I know my suggestion to rewrite the Bible would light the fires that are burning with such intensity. The fires have reached such high intensity that they are almost unquenchable. Nor should they be quenched.

The suggestion to rewrite the Bible is not my concern alone. Also in this crucial field is R.A. KANZIRA of Uganda.

This "colleague" (in The Ugandian Daily - May 24, 1991) wrote:

> **"The Bible is deficient. First of all the Old Testament is nothing but Jewish mythology and legend; its bits and pieces from Israel's history. The heart of the New Testament is the gospels.The gospels read like legend too on their own confession'according to ...'. Legend, yes. The effectiveness of Legends generally depend on the originality and creativeness of the narrator". 1**

He goes on to say:

> **"If the Bible, first the Old Testament is to make sense then it must be rewritten or infused with world history into which humanity will not be divided into chosen and foreign. Justification of evils like Zionism will have no palce in it". 2**

This analysis is precise. The concept of the choseness of Israel sounds like a little baby claiming monopoly of God's love. The references to other nations outside Israel are merely ways to describe God's relations wth Israel. In the book of Amos is is said:

"You only have I known of all the families of the earth"

(Amos 3:20)

This relationship between God and Israel dominate the Old Testament. If the Bible is to be more meaningful in this world the idea of choseness must be exposed and exploded. God is God of all peoples. He is a universal God and not the property of any one people. God cannot be a tribal animal. He is not a prisoner of culture but a liberator of it.

The hallow notion of the chosen race reached its Zenith in the 10th and 19th centuries when the so called social gospel clergy argued for the preservation of the Aglo-Saxon race.

In Thomas F Gossette's Race: The history of an idea in America p. 178/9 the Rev. Josiah Strong is quoted as saying:

"Far from lamenting the gradual disappearance of the American Indian, for example, we should see in his   extinction merely the reflection of the will of God in preparing the land for a better race, the Anglo-Saxons. Similarly, the troubles of the native peoples over the wolrd - as vexing as they might be - were merely local manifestations of a cosmic process, the replacing of inferior with superior stock. Just as strong was able to reconcile the theory of eveolution, the struggle for existance, and the survival of the fittest with an optimistic Protestant theology, so he was able to view the ascendancy and decline of races as part of the providence of God.

The idea that the nonwhite races might best fulfil the will of God simply by disappearing was not, of course, invented by Strong, not was it wholly the consequence of theology conditioned by Social Darwinism. "God cast out the heathen to make room for his people", one Puritan divine explained, referring to the sourious claims of the dispossessed Indians.

Another Puritan discovered "the special interposition of Providence in reducing by disease the Indians in Massachusetts from thirty thousand to three thousand".

Probably with his tongue in his cheek, Benjamin Franklin later expressed a rather similar idea, declaring in his Autobiography that rum was "the appointed means" of fulfilling "the design Providence to extirpate the savages in order to make room for cultivatore of the earth.

Likewise, the early English colonialist had thought of themselves as a chosen people long before the laws of biology were invoked to justify their superiority. The Puritans frequently compared their relationship to God to that of the Israelites of old. In the American Revilution, the phrase was revived to induce patriotism among the colonists. After the war, the theme of an "American Israel" formed the keynote of sermon delivered in 1783 by Ezra Stiles, president of Yale. Two years later Jefferson proposed that the seal of the United States should represent the children of Israel led by a pillar of light. In 1787 Timothy Dwight referred frankly to Americans a "this chosen race'.

There is need to realize that there was once a time when the Bible did not contain both Old and New Testament. In other words, faith in God precedes the writting of the Bible. People sustained their faith without the Bible. The Bible is a late phenomenon in the history of Israel. There is nothing magical about it.

The Bible is obvioulsly not a single book but a collection of books. Exegetical works on the Bible reveal that these books were composed over an indeterminate period of many centuries in three languages: Hebrew, Aramic and Greek. The authors of these books include both men of considerable learning and men of very little.

One may well ask, in view of all that has been said, in what sense, if any, can we justifiable speak without qualification of the Bible as the word of God. It used to be fashionable to believe that the Bible was written by men inspired by God and hence are holy scriptures. According to Deuteronomy, Moses wrote under divine inspiration:

"And it came to pass, when Moses had made an end of writting the words of this law in a book, until they were finished...." (Deut .31:24)

These authors were believed to be devinely illuminated for this purpose. Some Jews believed the Old Testament was authored by The spirit of God. Did God use his hands or his mouth to write the Bible? And in what language? This was the extreeme attitude Taken by the Swiss Confession of the 17th century - that the Hebrew manuscript of the Bible was inspired not only with regard to consonents but also to the vowel points. This unique authority of the Bible was never challenged until 19th century with the rise of mordern sciences. Such Biblicism is not helpful because the Bible has some inaccuracies and infelicities. The Bible is not literally inerrable.

The scope and content of both the OT an NT have been the subject of controversy. It is abundantly clear that the authors of the Bible utilized the material from oral traditions. These are recollections of the past handed down from generation to generation by word of mouth and are commonly known in societies in which they relate. Oral tradition is particularly important to non literate societies because it is the major way of keeping their history. The traditions are handed in many forms such as stones, oems, songs, folk tales etc.

However oral tradition has got it's own pitfalls/limitations. It depends on memory - how much the society remembers. Tradition is liable to distortion. A chief can fabricate the achievements of his predecessor so as to bolster his lineage. Therefore it is important for the historian to study the history of society prior to it's tradition. Traditions can be manipulated to fit into the present political and economic system of the society. Moreover people usually remember big events and not small ones. It is difficult to ascertain the chronology of events from oral tradition. Oral tradition should be corroborated by other sources of history otherwise its authenticity remains doubtful.

Jeffery writes:

> **"The story of growth of Hebrew literature is in no fundamental way different from that of the growth of literature among other peoples. Everywhere the beginnings of national literature are oral. As the people attain to literacy there is the tendency to put this national literature - the tales of origins, the annals of the kings, the deeds of the heroic age, the oracles of the shrines, the priestly liturgies, the popular religious songs, the wisdom of sages, and so forth - into written form". 3**

The point I have been arguing is that the Bible is the result of human decision selecting the writtings circulating in Israel and also the respect to the canonization of the NT. In this process of canonization some writtings were excluded. This is corroborated in the Gospel of John:

> "And there are also many other things which Jesus did, the which, if they should be written every one, I suppose that even the world itself could not contain the books that should be written". (John 21:25) . 4

Edgar Goodspeed writes:

> "The disputed books which Eusebius listed as "rejected" were the Acts of Paul, the Shepherd, the Revelation of Peter, the Letter of Barnabas, the Teaching of the Apostles. In referring to the Revelation of John, after acknowedging it "if it seem proper", he adds, "which some reject, but which some class with the accepted books" .5

> He has another list of books definitely heretical, such as the Gospel of Peter, the Gospel of Thomas, the Traditions of Mathias, the Acts of Andrew, and the Acts of John. His objection to these books was that they were not of apostolic origin, such origin being decided on the basis of use by earlier church writers and freedom from schismatic bias". 6

One might argue with some justification that what we call the Bible today is a Bible minus. It is incomplete. It is of paramount importance that the Bible be rewritten or if you like a new exercise in canonization.

According to Arthur Jeffrey:

> "The writtings assembled in such sacred books [Bible] are of various kinds, some historical, some didactic, some hortatory, some perhaps magical, but they gain their authority because the community feels that in them is enshrined something that is of vital significancefor the practice of the religion whose sacred books they are". 7

The same biblical scholar submits that with the passage of time there is:

"the possibility of adding to them already existing authetic material at some future time other writtings in which once again the sure voice of religious authority was heard, nor indeed of the adding to them of historical records, or memorials of the past of the community, without which much of the meaning of the word of prophecy might be lost" . 8

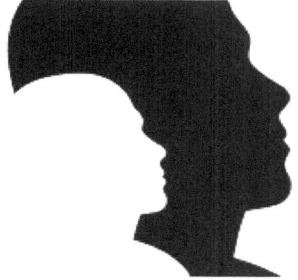

The so-called spirit-inspired authors were human being. Their points of view and modes of expressing their ideas determined the outcome of the Bible. Historians are of the viewpoint "that a canon of scripture is not something given, but something humanly devised" and thus liable to distortions. 9

It is not clear when and how the earliest assembling of sacred writings in Hebrew came about. II Kings 22 is a pointer to the existance of these collections. Perhaps the arrangement of the OT into law, the prophets and the Hagiograpphy may reveal the stages in the History of the canonization of the Old Testament. Generally many so-called sacred writings were assembled quite early in the history of Israel and were canonized later.

The name canon (measuring rod or rule) is usually applied to describe the books that were accepted by the assembling of rabbis at Jamnia around AD 90 or 100 under the leadership of Rabbi Akiba. It was at this assembly that the disputed song of Solomon and of ecclesiastes were included in the canon. This Hebew canon did not include the additions of Jeremiah, Esther and Daniel. These three additions are found in the septuagint (Greek canon). The Hebrew canon also rejected Tobit, Judith, Wisdom, Ecclesiastics, Brauch and the books of maccabees.

The Dead Sea Scrolls reveal that by about the 4th century BC the Pentateuch and the Prophets were canonized. Some books in the Hagiography were accepted while others were still in dispute until the assemble at Jamnia.

The New Testament refers to some books that do not belong to any canon. For example it refers to the book of Enock. This led some scholars to postulate that the NT is built on a double foundation. They argue that the Epistle to the Hebrews utilized the septuagint canon. On the other hand the rest of the NT is built on the narrower Palestinian canon. Though this argument is not exhaustive it points on the incoompleteness of the Bible.

The early fathers of the christian church did not clearly know the canon of the OT. According to Eusebuis Melito of Sardis (2nd century) inquired among Eastern teachers concerning the scope of their canon. 10. The catalogue of Athanisuis (4th century) omits Esther. The canon was not clearly defined in the first four centuries of the Christian era.

Writtings which bore "memories of the Apostles" were automatically accepted in the NT canon. These are the writtings that bore the names of apostles. Other writings which were compiled by the associates of disciples were also accepted. Eusebius says that some writings were accepted almost universally as part of the canon, others were disputed before being incorporated and still others were eventually rejected. The authenticity of the epistle to the Hebrews was questioned.

It might have been accepted in the orient section of the church but rejected in the occident. Also in this category are the epistle of James, I Peter and II Peter. The letter of Jude was only found in the Muratorian canon (in the west) but rejected elsewhere. The book of Revelation was hotly disputed before it was finally canonized. Apocalyptic literature was associated with the Montanist movements and this suspicious Eusebius and Athanasius agree that by the Middle of the 4th century the disputed books were approaching universal approval. 11. His canon appeared for the first time in the 39th festival letter of Athanasius AD 367. 12

The Early Fathers played a crucial role in the acceptance and rejection of early writings. The Bible has been translated into over 1000 languages. A close analysis of a new translation reveal that some well-known passages might be missing from it. The basis for leavig out some passages is questionable.

All that has been said so far show that the early history of christianity was characterised by canonisation of some sacred writings. It is high time we learn something from the acumulated experience of the church. To cling tanaciously to tradition in an unimaginative way, as we are doing, is tokill tradition. Tradition guards against subjectivism such as the one which misguides Zionism. We must be creators of tradition and not its victims.

There are some notorious verses in the Bible which must be uprooted. According to the so-called covenant with Abraham God is said to have uttered:

"And I will establish my covenant between me and you and your descendants after you throughout their generations for an everlasting covenant, to be God to you and to your   descendants after you.

And I will give you, and to your descendants after you the land of your sojournings, all the land of Canaan, for an everlasting possession and I will be their God" (Gen, 17:7-8)

This verse, among many others, affords Israel the most favoured status. It gives the picture of a discriminatory God. A God of injustice who condones hegemonism and agression.

Deutronomy 13: 6-10 is one of the most notorious passages in the Bible. It encourages the killing of worshippers of other Gods other that the God of Israel. The fact of the matter is that this is the same God the Istralites aretrying to possess tenaciously. It paints the picture of a hooligan God who loves punishing, destroying and annihilating. Our God is a God of mercy and kindness and compassion.

The above verses depict a God who is in

captivity _ a God who confines himself within the boundaries of Israel. This is tanatamount to limiting His Greatness. Attempts should be made through rewriting the Bible, to univesalize God. Revelation is not for Jews alone. Our God is discernible in all nations, Canada, Romania, India, Australia, Zimbabwe, to mention just a few. Every religion is an embodiment of the drama of God meeting man. There is only one infallible God discernible throught the world. It is totally misleading to say Christianity is the convergence of all religious development. Theologizing in Africa, just as in other parts of the world must take into account the peoples own traditional religious practices. God is discirnible in African traditional religious as in any other. We can encounter Christ in Africa in the same way Jews would do in Palestine.

It was within the broader understanding of the plurality of religions that I mention Mbuya Nehanda. It caused a stir I know. I equated Mbuya Nehanda with Abraham and not Jesus. The universalization of the Bible is never intended to change the content of the Gospel. Jesus is God. Mbuya Nehanda is not and Abraham is not. I believe from Mbuya Nehanda's life we can extract some important religious lessons as we do from Abraham. It is the religious practices which must be incorporated into Christianity. Such religious practices drawn from all over the world will enrich Christianity. Many nations have got rich religious insights. And hence there is need to rewrite the Bible so that the Bible will have soe universal ethos. We must expand the frontiers of religious excavation to encompas the whole world and search for eveidence of God's revelation in the various religious shrines. We cannot afford to make God a prisoner of the so called holy land. God's revelation is limitless and can be experienced across human frontiers. What is holy about the soil of Israel? And what is profane about the soil of Zimbabwe or any other country for that matter? What is the difference between Jerusalem and Harare? Absolutely none, perhaps the weather, or oppression and freedom.

Jewish sonety is patrilineal and this determined the outcome of the canon. The Bible portrays women as objects through which men manipulate their transactions. This is catogorically reflected in the Pualine letter to the Corinthians:

"As in all churches of the saints, the women should keep silent in the churches. For they are not permitted to speak, but should be subordinate, as even the law says. If there is anythig they desire to know, let them ask their husbands at home. For it is shameful for woman to speak in church". (I Cor 14: 34-35)

Women find terrible impasse in the Bible. These two neferous verses, inter alia, regard women as perpertual minors. The Bible is replete with uncouth and negative sentiments against women. The good news for all progressive minds is that we have already rewritten the Bible. It is rewritten in the form of allowing women on our pulpits. Who knows - We might have a female Pope soon. We have rewritten the Bible without saying so.

All we need is qualified personnel to consider re-writting the Bible. These scholars will excavate religious shrines throughout the world. Religious shrines might be repositories of religious insights which will help is in rewriting the Bible. These scholars will determine whether Mbuya Nehanda, Chilembwe, Bhuda, Mohammed, Kimbangu, to mention just these, have something to offer.

A rewritten universal Bible will provide Christians with an authentic and more meangful Bible. I urge Christians not to be emotional. The Bible must be freed from Zionist encasement and reveal universal ethos. Consequently Israel will stop its extravagant claims of holiness and choseness. Since God is discernible world wide I have no qualms to submit that the Zambezi river, Save River, Nile River, Niger River, Mississipi and millions more are as holy as the Jordan river. You can as well be baptized in any. There is nothing special about the Jordan now. We have a responsibility to rewrite the Bible and the sooner we do so the better.

The question of re-wiriting the Bible is nothing new, this is an ongoing process. We would be betraying millions of Christians throughout the world were we to fail to exercise our obligation of our ciritical review of the major sources of our faith, a critical uppraisal of scripture can only lead to enlightened and rational faith.

REFERENCES

1. R.A. KANZIRA of Uganda. This "colleague" (in The Ugandian Daily - May 24, 1991)

2. IBID

3. JEFFERY A, "the canon of the Old Testament", in The Interpreters Bible, p.32

4. JOHN 21:25

5. EDGAR GOODSPEED, THE INTERPRETERS BIBLE, P66

6. IBID

7. IBID, p33

8. IBID

9. ENCYCOPEDIA BRITTANICA, Vol. 3. 1768, p. 576

10. IBID

11. IBID, p.578

12. IBID

IMAGES

1. Banana Family Photo Library [1972 - 2019]

2. Royalty Free Images, [https://www.tokkoro.com/3115858-architecture_austria_building_catholic_christian_church_historically_house-of-worship_linz_martin-ch.html]

OTHER PUBLISHED WORKS BY CANAAN BANANA

➡**The woman of my imagination Unknown Binding – 1980**

by Canaan Banana (Author)

Product details

Unknown Binding: 150 pages

Publisher: Mambo Press (1980)

Language: English

ASIN: B0006ECGH0

➡**In search of human justice: Martin Luther King lecture delivered at Wesley Theological Seminary, 22nd October, 1981 (Martin Luther King lectures) Unknown Binding – 1981**

by Canaan Banana (Author)

Product details

Series: Martin Luther King lectures

Unknown Binding: 28 pages

Publisher: s.n.] (1981)

Language: English

ASIN: B0007C06PU

➡**The theology of promise: The dynamics of self-reliance Paperback – 1982**

by Canaan Banana (Author)

Product details

Paperback: 156 pages

Publisher: College Press (1982)

Language: English

ISBN-10: 0869253794

ISBN-13: 978-0869253793

Shipping Weight: 1.7 pounds

➡Towards a socialist ethos: Socialism without socialists is capitalism Paperback – 1987

by Canaan Banana (Author)

Product details

Paperback: 60 pages

Publisher: College Press (1987)

Language: English

ISBN-10: 0869258249

ISBN-13: 978-0869258248

Shipping Weight: 1.1 pounds

➡Christianity and the struggle for socialism in Zimbabwe today Unknown Binding – 1988

by Canaan Banana (Author)

Product details

Unknown Binding: 12 pages

Publisher: Ministry of Information, Post and Telecommunications of the Government of Zimbabwe (1988)

Language: English

ASIN: B0007BR9BU

➡Turmoil and Tenacity Zimbabwe 1890 - 1990 Paperback – 1989

by Canaan Banana (Editor)

Product details

Paperback: 396 pages

Publisher: College Press Publishers Pvt Ltd; First Edition edition (1989)

Language: English

ISBN-10: 086925992X

ISBN-13: 978-0869259924

Package Dimensions: 8.4 x 5.8 x 0.7 inches

Shipping Weight: 1.1 pounds (View shipping rates and policies)

➡**The gospel according to the ghetto Unknown Binding – 1990**

by Canaan. Banana (Author)

Product details

Publisher: Mambo Press (1980)

ASIN: B007FRV2P8

➡**African theology in post colonial Africa : an African approach from the perspective of the eleventh anniversary of Zimbabwe's independence Unknown Binding – 1991**

by Canaan. Valparaiso University. Banana (Author)

Product details

Unknown Binding

Publisher: Valparaisio [sic] University (1991)

ASIN: B007HGK2BM

➡**Come and share: An introduction to Christian theology Paperback – 1991**

by Canaan Banana (Author)

Product details

Paperback: 119 pages

Publisher: Mambo Press; Revised edition (1991)

Language: English

ISBN-10: 0869224956

ISBN-13: 978-0869224953

Package Dimensions: 7.7 x 5 x 0.4 inches

Shipping Weight: 4 ounces

➡Politics of repression and resistance: Face to face with combat
theology Paperback – 1996

by Canaan Banana (Author)

Product details

Paperback: 335 pages

Publisher: Mambo Press (1996)

Language: English

ISBN-10: 0869226509

ISBN-13: 978-0869226506

Shipping Weight: 1.1 pounds

ACKNOWLEDGEMENTS

This book is a direct extract from the original Case Study document presented by
the late Professor Canaan Sodindo Banana at a Seminar for Religious Studies,
Classics and Philosophy at the University of Zimbabwe on June 14 1991. This was
following Professor Banana's attendence of a conference in Hatfield where he
discussed the task of African (third world) theologians on the Middle East Question.

His suggestion to rewrite the Bible at the time was met with strong resistence and
emotional reactions from the generality of the public before they even had the
opportunity to interogate the view points the professor was trying to bring to the
fore. This is why I (Nathan Banana) in consultation with close family have decided
to make the full study available for public reading and academic reference where
needed.